A Book of Smallness

Don Schaeffer

ISBN: 978-93-6354-369-0

First Edition: 2025
Rs. 200/-

Cyberwit.net
HIG 45 Kaushambi Kunj, Kalindipuram
Allahabad - 211011 (U.P.) India
http://www.cyberwit.net
Tel: +(91) 9415091004
E-mail: info@cyberwit.net

Printed at Repro India Limited.

Contents

A Visit to an Intimate Far Away Near

Sir Rotifer
is a soldier
in the water army,
a giant lobster
when all others are
tiny snakes and shell lost clams.
This is one of the
smallest of the mighty
and the oldest of the
children. Hail to the king.
the disorganizing
molecules to keep
marching even as death
kept them loose and
scattered. The tiny
motion death permitted
could not bind them.

The Time Line

Love only takes
a few minutes,
maybe just
a few hours a day.
Meassured against
the scale of life
with all the colors
in that list
of moments,
the two-eyed stereo
solitary moments
are life.
I waited for you
most of the time
and got to know you,
amd found you,
and lost you,
renewed you
more than I
touched you.
It just seemed like,
and I summarize it as,
I loved you.

With Hands Upstretched

This tells you how spoiled I am,
how far away I am from now.
What is solid in the world I have
changed to gas and dust, I have
taken down the spreading fabric,
I no longer reach for what.
has retreated inside the door.
It's wearer no longer speaks..
The cold hits me directly now.
There is no garment.
I miss what has vanished,
even though she was rarely mine.
I am disappointed in God.
not speaking, unless
this is His speech.

The Birth

The words were
just at the edge of
nonsense, just beyond
comedy, almost
ready to be
torn in disgrace
from the page.

I took pity for the words,
for myself, for that time,
those moments,
those years
when I did not
discard them.

The Brain of a Spider

I was reading today
about the froth
in a spider's brain,
so small and so fierce.
There are no machines in there
just grains of magic
that come from lumps
of space so far away
locked threads
slowly drying,
hungers and death machines.
We drive them away.
They don't deserve
the fear they make.
But I'm sure
some god is laughing.

Swan Lake

At the end of the day
when there is nothing left
I let the dressed up
dancers in.

They come with smile and song,
glad to add
flesh to their dreams,
that is not flesh.

At the end of the day
with light dreams singing,
I smile, at the edge of a laugh,
and the dancers are busy

when I look for dancers.

Televised Metaphysics

I know you die
but is that
the same as
being alive just
quieter, perhaps,
and having a
different smell,
when everyone
becomes a stranger
and evil becomes
more real?
I saw it on tv.
And I thought.

A Hole in Death

He comes to me at night,
unsuspected, pops cheerfully
onto my bed
just to disobey. His fur
is soft like cream.
I would not call him
beautiful, not even
charming. He has a
mean, self reliant look
and he is stuborn and
persistant. He purrs
that gravelly music. He is
a purveyor of mystery
here on my planet
but from another world.
The only word for it
is love.

The Day

Whisps of lace
brush under the wind.
That is the day.
Then I rest. It gets
dark. Fragile bits of
lace, torn from
the great skirt,
floating away
finally reach the ground.
Then I have to sleep,
soundless. The words
are cast away scraps,
paste and ink,
little blots of memory
and wanting
float in silence.
The future is a
picture frame.

A Vision

One day
there was someone
with whom I
almost had paradise.
It would have been
brief but would have been
real. The figure of her
lives in my mind
with broken strokes
of relief and fear.
She is mine now,
pure image,
a being of hope and dread
just for an hour
many years ago,
lacing strings of memory,
more vivid than life, that
still generates dreams.

The Pillow

Seeing this problem
when it is
past midnight
just off the path to dreams,
seeing this problem
on route away from sleep,
where sleep is
a form of sanity,
both in this world and out,
collecting words
and hoping for sentences
where sleep
does not create
sentences.

The Introductory Strains of Something New

It's not a message
but a hint. The melody
becomes song-like,
even though
I can't make out
the words. It wants,
not to hide
but to melt, unformed.
Darkness and fog,
a quiet confusion
masks something new
that doesn't look new,
something that
reminds me in silence.
Whatever was in the past
just leaks into the future.
Everything is soft,
and wants to rest.

Khan's Giselle

I woke up today
with something
broken and I said,
at last. From the fog
I tried
to polish my eyes.
Of course, fear, my adviser
was not helpful.
Maybe I broke something
when I tried so hard to learn.
The gates to the future
may be slowly
closing, as in the final
ballet scene
where the dancers
slowly lower the curtain.

America

He wakes up in the morning
suddenly
as a cockroach.
That
is a strange inconvenience
and he was planning
for an ice cream dinner.
Being ugly
is a shame,
living under
the same
sun as hours before,
wanting his old
face back.
When fate
is stubborn,
never relenting or
compromising,
he just
cries.

A Silly Moment

I am in the mood to cry.
It just feels good.
I am a lover of outburst,
not sad but ejaculated, un-holdable.
Please give me one
and make me worthy of it.
The silent, withheld streets and books
keep me from breathing and I
don't know how much time
remains. I join the world
in waiting.

Imperfection

So many of those
precious moments just
go away, lost. My life is just
a few minutes with a
bunch of grey shadows.

It was such a
long time. I waited and
pondered
and vanished and
reappeared and
never appeared again
and said goodbye or
didn't say goodbye.

And wrapped it all up
and let pieces leak.
Such a long time and
passing so quickly.
And missed some
warm hands who
chose something else.

The Rhyme at the End

There are writers who
call it poetry and laugh.
I am not a laugher. I am
sad. I am reaching out for
things that aren't there.
And nobody knows.
The walls are cold
except for the scratch marks.
And the day ends
when the lights go out
and nobody looks
in spite of the fact that
the night has the brightest lights
and sleepless eyes. And the
world is so open even
with the lies. And the
years are full of fading
and beggars.

Nothing Tries to Grasp My Hand.

I wake up today
in glory. I know
the sun and the day
all friends and
joy is near, not always
by my side but speaking.
I draw pictures and make
warm, continuous plans.

But then there is night,
broken between warnings
and cautions. It is
a space between me
and Nothing. And Nothing
shivers beside me.
Nothing tries to grasp my hand.
And Nothing has no fingers.
How will I greet Nothing
when it comes? It does not
say hello.

State of the Race

I have removed the covering
and so far nobody looked.
Ha. We are pretty
sophisticated in this world.
There is hardly anything
that can amaze us,
especially not things
that are hidden. They just
make us laugh and that
simply hurts. I ask
what can make us gasp?
We just want to laugh.
I emerge with face
covered in sweat. And
I know I have failed to amaze.

Contmporary Life

Why does it matter
that she is far away?
Why does it matter
that she is made of chalk?
Tiny lights speak,
don't need fingers.
Flesh is on Earth
but not in the sky.

Life Instinct in Drowned Leaf Cells

As if they
want to keep their form
and try to command
the disorganizing
molecules to keep
marching even as death
kept them loose and
scattered. The tiny
motion death permitted
could not bind them.

A Visit to an Intimate Far Away Near

Sir Rotifer
is a soldier
in the water army,
a giant lobster
when all others are
tiny snakes and shell lost clams.
This is one of the
smallest of the mighty
and the oldest of the
children. Hail to the king.
the disorganizing
molecules to keep
marching even as death
kept them loose and
scattered. The tiny
motion death permitted
could not bind them.

The Time Line

Love only takes
a few minutes,
maybe just
a few hours a day.
Meassured against
the scale of life
with all the colors
in that list
of moments,
the two-eyed stereo
solitary moments
are life.
I waited for you
most of the time
and got to know you,
amd found you,
and lost you,
renewed you
more than I
touched you.
It just seemed like,
and I summarize it as,
I loved you.

With Hands Upstretched

This tells you how spoiled I am,
how far away I am from now.
What is solid in the world I have
changed to gas and dust, I have
taken down the spreading fabric,
I no longer reach for what.
has retreated inside the door.
It's wearer no longer speaks..
The cold hits me directly now.
There is no garment.
I miss what has vanished,
even though she was rarely mine.
I am disappointed in God.
not speaking, unless
this is His speech.

The Birth

The words were
just at the edge of
nonsense, just beyond
comedy, almost
ready to be
torn in disgrace
from the page.

I took pity for the words,
for myself, for that time,
those moments,
those years
when I did not
discard them.

www.ingramcontent.com/pod-product-compliance
Ingram Content Group UK Ltd.
Pitfield, Milton Keynes, MK11 3LW, UK
UKHW041317190726
13845UKWH00025B/325

9 789363 543690